I0015791

The Blueprint To Hacking

Beginners Guide to Ethical Computer Hacking!

By: Cyber Punk Architects

Table Of Contents

Book 1

The Blueprint To Hacking

Book 2

Computer Programming Language: The Blueprint

Respective authors own all copyrights not held by the publisher.

Legal Notice:

Disclaimer Notice:

By reading this document, the reader agrees that under no circumstances are we responsible for any losses, direct or indirect, which are incurred as a result of the use of information contained within this document, including, but not limited to, —errors, omissions, or inaccuracies.

About CyberPunk Architects

Computer programming doesn't have to be complicated. When you start with the basics its actually quite simple. That is what Cyberpunk Architects are all about. We take pride in giving people the *blueprint* for everything related to computer programming and computer programming languages. We include Python programming, Raspberry Pi, SQL, Java, HTML and a lot more.

We take a sophisticated approach and teach you everything you need to know from the ground up. Starting with a strong base is the only way you will truly master the art of computer programming. We understand that it can be challenging to find the right way to learn the often complex field of programming especially for those who are not tech savvy. Our team at Cyberpunk Architects is dedicated to helping you achieve your goals when it comes to computer programming.

We are here to provide you with the *blueprint* to give you a strong foundation so you can build on that and go into any area of programming that you wish. Our architects are comprised of professionals who have been in the industry of information technology for decades and have a passion for teaching and helping others especially through our books. They are friendly, experienced, knowledgeable computer programmers who love sharing their vast knowledge with anyone who has an interest in it.

We look forward to getting a chance to work with you soon. Here at Cyberpunk Architects, you can always be sure that you are working with right people. Allow us take care of your needs for learning computer programming. If you have any questions about the services that we are providing, please do not hesitate to get in touch with us right away.

Check out all of our books at:

Bit.ly/Cyberpunkbooks

As a THANK YOU for purchasing our books we want to give you **a free bonus**. **A quick guide on how to get started with programming**. This book covers the basics of what you want to know to get started.

Free Bonus!

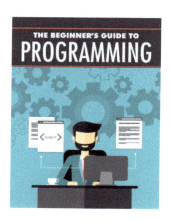

Programing can be hard but it doesn't have to be! Take this free PDF guide to understand some of the basics of programming

Download the free guide:

bit.ly/cpfreeguide

Introduction

With today's high level of technological culture
and massive development of information
technology, there is no surprise many people
see their future in this field of industry. This
type of science, information science is desirable
and available to broad masses of people. By
knowing the real power of information
technology, you will be able to manipulate,
store and study many different types of data
from the comfort of your home.

In the world, there are many undergraduate
degree programs preparing students to work in
this field of industry on many different levels.
IT specialists work for huge companies and are
responsible for network administration and
software development, increasing productivity
and efficiency.

On the other hand, there is huge subculture

involving people who are accessing online databases, manipulating and overcoming limitations of the software. By overcoming the obstacles and limitations of programming systems, you will be able to engage in advanced studies of software and operating systems. You will enter into a different world of information technology.

This book is about ethical computer hacking, so we will discuss hacking only in an ethical manner. Hacker ethic allows you to manipulate software in no harmful way, to share information to the world that is not damaging in any way. This guide will teach you how to access computers and information that can benefit you and others as well.

We all know that knowledge should be shared, especially knowledge that can be helpful and can improve our personal knowledge. Information should be available to everybody, and all information should be free. Today computers are life changing and take a huge part in everybody's life. This ethical beginner's guide to hacking computer will be your card into the power of information technology.

There is a common goal, many principles and values of hacker ethic are based on this common goal. By using the knowledge of hacking, you will be able to create something completely new and interesting. You will be able to access computers, learn about operating systems and share information to the world. You will see limitless opportunities in the information sector and be amazed by the greatness and power of one single information.

Ethical ideas and values of this subculture have constructive goal, and there is always feeling of right and wrong present. Only ethical hacking is right and no damaging in any way. In order to overcome obstacles of hacking, first of all, you will need to be online. Besides being online you will need operating system Linux, most of the internet sites run Linux operating system.

I will later explain how to use Linux Terminal. You need to have point to point protocol internet connection. Most of DLS connections are fortunately point to point protocol. If you don't have PPP (point to point protocol) contact your internet service provider and tell them you are interested in getting PPP.

All of these steps will be explained later step by step, but you should know that hacking isn't easy job. It demands constant learning and adoption of new knowledge. Learning and discovering is an essential thing when it comes to hacking. It will take you a certain number of hours on computer each day.

Before going into world of hacking, you should be familiar with programming languages and have certain programming skills. There are many programming languages, and I recommend Python because It is simple and easy to use. There are great tutorials about programming with Python, so you don't need to spend extra money on books. Besides Python later you should be learning other programming languages like C and C++, they are very difficult to learn, but at some point, you will be able to use them after learning the basics of Python.

We will discuss these basic steps later in details. First, you need to know there are many different types of hackers and many reasons why people enter the world of hacking. You should be familiar with these types of hackers even though this is such a stereotypical view.

1. **Script Kiddie** is the type I am mentioning first. This is normally amateur hacker who breaks into people's

computers and have poor knowledge of information technology. Script Kiddie use prepackaged automatic scripts and software created by real hackers. They are copying codes from these automatic scripts; they just download prepared software in order to put a virus or something else harmful. Basically, they watch YouTube tutorials on how to use these scripts. They flood an IP address with huge amount of information, and it collapses.

2.   **White Hat** is known as ethical hacker. Many of White Hat hackers have college degree in IT technology and security. They have non-malevolent and no damaging purpose. They are helping people fight against other hackers, help them remove viruses or PenTest companies. White Hat is by all standards ethical and moral programmer.

3.   **Black Hat**are the third type of hackers, commonly known as crackers. They surf the internet and discover weak frameworks. They are using basic and common hacking techniques to steal money and information from banks and companies with weak security systems.

4.   **Grey Hat** is another type of hacker.bGrey Hat is breaking into computers with weak security, breaking into PC frameworks. Gray Hat hackers are using many different strategies in order to extort Mastercard, many other types of vandalism and various types of information stealing.

5.   **Green Hat**are hackers really into hacking. They want to learn and discover always, and that is why they may be asking many basic questions. They are

listening with great devotion and
curiosity.

Elite hacker is above the average in the hacking
world, really devoted with great social status
among the others. They are treated as special in
the subculture of hacking. They are masters of
discovering and inventing new things. Masters
with solid reputation among the people, cream
of the hacker world.

These are the most relevant types of hackers.
This guide is about ethical hacking so you
should use your knowledge only for moral and
ethical purposes.

Chapter 1: How To Setup Your New Hacking Environment

It is impossible to learn everything about hacking; there is huge amount of information on the computers. People usually tend to specialize in one specific field when it comes to hacking such as software development, computer security or networking. It is a bit early for you as a beginner to think about specializing in any of these fields. You should first learn basic techniques and strategies when it comes to hacking. Later in future, you will have clearer mind about your possibilities.

Discovering and knowing what is going on inside the computer system is an essential thing, this is common goal of all hackers. By knowing what is going on inside the system, you will be able to manipulate and modify information for better. You are going to create something completely new that fits your needs. Learning about hacking is gaining access into powerful system of information and technology.

Knowledge will always be the most powerful thing, and power has been used both in good and wrong things. We will just focus on knowledge for moral and ethical purposes that benefit many people.

Here are the steps you should take to get started:

1. You have already taken the first step into the world of hacking by showing an interest and curiosity to learn about hacking.

2. Like I mentioned before, the second step is knowing the basics of programming languages. Programming skills and techniques are going to be the most valuable

you have for hacking. A programming language is designed to give instructions to the machines, especially computers. With the programming languages, you can create different programs and control the behavior of the computer. You should start with something simple like creative website or create application for smartphone.

Where and which programming languages to learn?

On the internet, there are many great tutorials about using programming languages. You can watch video tutorial as well. You shouldn't forget about library. There you can find tons of books about programming and networking. Besides video tutorials and books, there are plenty sites on the internet with step by step guides about programming.

- Java is one of the longest influential

programming languages, great for beginners. It lets you think like real hacker, to think logically. Besides Java I mentioned before Python, it is open and free to use. It will teach you really useful strategies, modularity, and indentation.

3. For the perfect hacking environment, you will need certain devices. Like I said before you have to be able to be online and have point to point protocol. If you don't have one you should contact your internet provider, but don't worry, almost every DLS internet connection has PPP. Other important things are you should have some knowledge about network ports, common network protocols, HTTP and you should know how each of these things works.

4. You will need operating system that is convenient for programming. Unix operating system is perfect and suitable for

hackers all over the world. Unix operating system can develop and create software that can be run on other systems as well. You can use a great number of software tools. Unix consists of many great utilities such as a master program kernel. Unix emerged as important learning and teaching tools when it comes to computer technology.

- Besides unix operating system, you will need shell account. A shell account is user account that runs on the remote server under the Unix operating system. It gives you access to a shell via different kinds of protocols. Shell accounts have been used for file storage, software development or web space.
- You will also need a Unix box. It is a computer that runs any of the several Unix operating systems like Linux. This term Unix box came in order to distinguish Unix operating system and

more common Windows operating system. Unix operating system and Unix computer are able to differentiate many different servers quickly. Unix computers are perfect for security administration as well as for hacking. The most important thing is that most internet websites are running Unix operating system.

- In order to obtain Unix operating system, you will have to buy one or get free versions. I recommend Linux operating system or BSD. Linux is more suitable for beginners because it is easy to use, so you should consider buying Linux first. You can buy Linux set online from many different sites. There are many free versions of Linux; you will just need to find someone with this operating system to burn it for your personal use. Don't worry, Linux is free for distribution, and it's not illegal to makes copies.

- When it comes to installing Linux operating system, don't worry, it is quite easy. You can find complete guides and video tutorials on the internet with the installation instructions. Just type into search engine Linux installation, you will get all of the information that you need.

Reminder: In order to hack and manipulate the software, you have to be able to be online using Linux operating system. Like I mentioned before, you need point to point protocol internet connection. Almost all of the DLS connections are point to point protocol, but on the other hand, dial-up is not PPP. If you have DLS connection, you are lucky, and there is no need to worry about anything. You are ready for some hacking.

5. After you get these stuff, it is time to pick books about Linux operating system or any other operating system you may be using. I recommend you books with step by step guides for beginners. Your local library has plenty of books about computer technology; it won't be a problem finding any particular one you need. For me personally, the best book about Linux is Running Linux written by Matt Welsh. It is really for beginners in computer technology. If you are maybe using other Unix versions of operating system, I warmly recommend any book from O'Reilly Collection. I find them perfect for beginners.

You have to keep in mind constantly that hacking is hard work, constant learning about information and computer science in different and intriguing ways. You just made your first step; you are intrigued by hacking world, you

28

want to know about manipulating software, creating something completely new from information you get. That is the most important step, wanting to know more. You should keep in mind that hacking is huge devotion, you will need to expand your limits and knowledge. The most important thing is learning, so you have to read a lot about information and computer technology, search online for your many questions, visit forums about hacking. After setting up perfect environment for hacking, we should start with basics.

Chapter 2: How To Use The Linux Terminal And Master Its Functions

As I mentioned before, Linus is Unix-like computer operating system; it is developed under the version of the free and open-source software. Unix operating systems are free for distribution and development. The most important component of Linux operating system is Linux kernel. Originally Linux was developed for personal use and computers, but since then Linux has been developing many other platforms, more than any other operating system. Today Linux is the most used operating system in the world, has the largest installed base of all operating systems and is leading operating system on many servers and desktop computers. Today many smartphones run Linux components and derivatives.

The greatest example of free and open-source software is absolutely the development of Linux operating system. Source codes may be distributed and modified by anyone by the certain terms and licenses. You can use find many popular mainstream Linux versions such as Fedora, Linux Mint or Ubuntu. You have plenty options. Besides these versions, you can find for free supporting utilities, large amount of applications and software supporting Linux operating system. All of these have supporting role in distribution's intended use.

Linux is high-level assembly, and programming language freely redistributed and with easy porting to any computer platform. For this reason, Unix-like operating system Linux quickly became adopted by academic circles and institutions. Today it is widely used and distributed all over the world. Linux is the result of the project of creating Unix-like operating system with completely free software. It is opponent to the Microsoft's monopoly in the desktop computer technology. Linux today is more used in the field of embedded systems and supercomputers.

Linux is modular operating system; device drivers are integrated or added like modules while the system is running. Some of the Linux components include C standard library, widget toolkits, and software libraries. This guide will help you and guide you through the Linux terminal commands and basics. Linux Terminal is really powerful tool, and you shouldn't be afraid to use it.

Learning the Linux basics is first and crucial step into the world of hacking. In this guide, we have to cover topics such as Linux command line and Linux executing commands. These are basics when it comes to the Linux operating system. You should familiarize yourself with the Linux Terminal emulator in the first place. It will become very easy to use when we pass through the basics first. It is needless to say you have to be able to connect to the Linux server.

At the very beginning, we should distinguish what the terminal emulator is. Terminal emulator is the program allowing the usage of terminal in a graphical environment. Today many people use operating system with graphical user interface and terminal emulator is an essential feature for Linux users. Besides Linux, you can find terminal emulator program in other operating systems such as Mac OS X and Windows. Here we are going to discuss Linux Terminal emulator.

You should be familiar with the shell. When it comes to the Linux, the shell is standing for command-line interface. The shell reads and interprets commands from the user. It reads script files and tells the operating system what to do with the obtained scripts. There are many widely used shells such as C shell or Bourne shell. Every shell has its own features, but many of the shells feature some same characteristics. Each shell function in the same way of input and output direction and condition-testing. Bourne-Again shell is the default shell for almost every Linux version.

Another important thing is knowledge of command prompt. The message of the day is the first thing you will see when you log in to server. It is message containing information about the version of Linux you a recurrently using. After the message of the day, you will be directed into the shell prompt known as command prompt. In the command prompt, you will give directions and tasks to the server. You will see information ate the shell prompt, and these information can be modified and customized by the users. In the command prompt, you are able to manipulate the information.

You may be logged into the shell prompt as root. In the Linux operating system, the root user is the special user who is able to perform administrative tasks and functions of the operating system. Super user account has permission to perform unrestricted commands to the server. As a super user, you have limitless powers when it comes to the manipulating commands given to the server. You will be able to give unrestricted administrative tasks and commands.

Besides shell prompt, we should discuss executing commands as well. You give commands to the server in the shell prompt. You specify the name of the files both as script of binary program. With the operating system Linux, there are already many utilities installed previously. These utilities let you navigate through the file system, install applications and configure the system. Giving tasks and commands in the shell prompt is called the process.

By giving directions in the command prompt, you are able to install software package and navigate through the system. When you are executing the commands in the foreground, you have to wait for the process to be finished before going to the shell prompt. This default way of commands being executed is case-sensitive including all names and files, commands and options. If something is not working as planned, you should double-check the spelling and case of all your commands.

You may have problems while connecting to the Linux server, online you can find solution to the problem with the connection. In order to execute the command free of arguments and options, you just simply type name of the command and press return. Commands like this, without arguments and options, behave differently from the commands with arguments. The behavior of the outcome varies from each command.

When it comes to the commands with arguments and options, accepting arguments and options can change the overall performance of the command. Every argument specifies and directs the command in a certain way. For example, a cd is the component of the command and arguments follows the certain command. Options that follows commands are known as flags.

Options are nothing more than special arguments directed in a certain way. They also affect and modify the behavior at the command prompt space. Same as arguments, options follow the commands and can contain more than one options for the same command. Options are single-character special arguments usually having descriptive character. Both arguments and options contain additional information about the commands and about each file and script. They can be combined into certain groups of options and arguments while running commands at the command prompt.

We should pay attention to the environment variables as well. Environment variables can change behavior of the commands and the ways of the command execution. First when you log in to server, default environment valuables will be set already according to configuration files. You can see at the command prompt all environment variables sessions by running env command. After running any command, next step is looking for path entry. The path will give you all the directions about the shell looking for executable programs and scripts.

From command prompt, you can retrieve the values of environment variables just by prefixing name of the variable with $character. By doing this, you will expand variable to its value. IF you see an empty string, you are probably trying to access variable which hasn't been set yet. In that case, you will get empty string.

Now that you are familiar with the environment variables you are able to set them. For setting environment variable you need to type variable name followed by an = sign. Finally, you should type the desired value. The original value of the variable will be overwritten if you are setting the existing environment variable and if the variable doesn't exist by doing this, it will be created. Command export allows you to export variables inherited during the process. To be more clear, you can use any script from the exported variable from current process.

When it comes to the referencing existing variables, you can always add directory at the end of the path command. You should keep in mind that modifying and adding environment variables in this particular way only sets the environment for your current session and any changes made will not be preserved for next sessions.

Chapter 3: How To Be Completely Anonymous Online Like The Pro's

Being hacker means breaking into the system, being individual who is modifying valuable information and sharing it with the world without certain authorization. Hacker gets into the system by the communication networks. Hacker essentially means computer programmer who can subvert any computer security. On the other side, there are hackers hacking with malicious purpose. These people are criminals, and they are illegally accessing computer systems. I mentioned before hackers stealing and entering into banks' and companies' computer security.

Hackers use their abilities and knowledge in computer science also good purposes as well. We are going to pay attention only to ethical and moral hacking. On the other hand, there is no surprise; hackers are disreputable. We heard about many cases in the past about stealing information which resulted in many accounts being compromised and many unauthorized transfers happen. Many banks and companies were targets and hit with the hacking attack. These attacks cost huge amount of money to both banks and companies, great amount of lost resources spent on investigation, more than stolen amount.

Hackers with malicious purposes besides stealing from banks and companies, usually steal peoples' personal information, online accounts especially social accounts and other personal files and data. When it comes to the ethical and moral hacking, you should keep in mind that you are always at risk to get caught. In this chapter, we are going to see how to be completely anonymous like a professional. Of course, keep in mind only ethical and moral hacking for good purposes is desirable hacking and any other purpose will not be discussed.

There are certain strategies and techniques how to hack like a professional and not get caught. Hackers like to get through many obstacles and penetrate into the computer system, and best way to do that is to be completely anonymous. Any other way is suspicious and may be dangerous. There are many restrictions while entering the computer system. An essential thing is being anonymous online and protecting your work. Hackers have to stay anonymous and not get traced by many tricks like using stronger passwords or using two-factor authentication.

How not to be caught and stay anonymous?

1. When it comes to the tips of being completely anonymous while hacking, the most important thing you can do is

try not use windows operating system. For the perfect hacking environment, you will need unix operating system which is perfect for hacking job. Getting Linux operating system and computer will be money good spent. Windows operating system is not good for hacking due to many holes that can be traced easily. These windows holes in the security may be deciding factor in spyware infecting and compromising your anonymity. You should definitely use other operating system security hardened system.

2.   The second thing you should pay attention is to avoid connecting to the internet directly. You can easily be tracked through your IP address. So if you want to avoid this, you should use VPN services which stand for virtual private network. The virtual private

network allows users to share and receive files and data while online through public networks like the internet. While you are online using virtual private network, you are connected as if your computer is directly connected to the private network. All of the applications you are running through a virtual private network can benefit in functionality and security. With a virtual private network, you are going to be able to surf the internet with great security and lower risk of being caught.

How does VPN help you stay anonymous?
In order to be connected to the virtual private network, you will need to connect to the proxy servers which have purpose of protecting your identity and location as well. However many sites on the internet are blocking access to the virtual private network technology in order to prevent unauthorized entering and wandering.

VPN is essentially point to point connection which is using other connections and virtual tunneling protocols. Many benefits are provided by using a virtual private network for a wide-area network.

When it comes to the hacking, VPN will let you create private tunnel, anyone who is trying to trace your IP address will only see the address of the virtual private network server, and you can choose any address in the world.

Which VPN to use?

When it comes to the virtual private network services, there are plenty of options. Some of the best software for secure and private browsing the internet are ExpressVPN, NordVPN, PureVPN and all of these are free to download. You should keep in mind before downloading VPN software that not all of these are created equal. Some of the VPN software may offer you top notch services while others can play fast with your files and data. Before buying and downloading any of the VPN software keep this in mind.

3.   TOR is network full of nodes which are routing your traffic. Directions of the nodes are behind and in front. Your direction onto normal internet connections is known as exit point. The most secure and the best way is to combine both virtual private network and TOR. In order to be anonymous while being connected to the internet, you should download free TOR software. TORsoftware is going to protect your personal data from network surveillance and help you defend against trafficking analysis. These types of network surveillance threaten all of your personal privacy and work against your freedom. TOR software will protect and secure

your internet connection and prevent other people from seeing sites you are visiting. The most important thing is that TOR software is completely free for downloading.

4.   Another one crucial thing when it comes to the hacking is email address. You should never use your email address while hacking. Instead of using your real email address, you should use one from the anonymous email service. Anonymous email service is letting their users send and receive emails from someone without any trace especially if you already have TOR software and virtual private network. When you go online every site is background checking your activities like google which is expecting you to share some of your personal information like email address or number.

Which email service software to get?

In order to set completely anonymous email address that can't be traced and without a connection to any server I recommend you download the software Hushmail's. Hushmail's is software very easy to use without any advertising, but it comes with the price, and on the other hand there is free version offering 25 MB of storage. If you don't want to pay extra money for the software, another great anonymous email service is software Guerilla Mail. Messages received in this mail are only temporary and will be available only for an hour.

Great way to stay anonymous and hide your email existence is website Mailinator, free and disposable. Whenever someone asks you for the email, you just make one up and sign into the Mailinator account and check received mail without leaving any traces. With the combination of the anonymous email service,

TOR software and accessing connection through the virtual private network you are almost invisible to the others. By doing this, you protected your personal information and defended from the third party sites which are tracking your IP address and location every time you go online.

5.   It may seem obvious, but you should never use Google while hacking. Google is constantly tracking sites that you are visiting and all of your online activities. Google is the most useful search engine, and there is certain way for you to use it without revealing your identity and personal information. You should use some of the services for preventing Google storing your IP address, records of your searches and cookies. I recommend you to use services such as StartPage or DuckDuck go which will prevent google from remembering your

online searches and history of your online activity. You will be able to search through the google without compromising your identity.

6.   Last but not least thing you should keep in mind is using public wireless connection. There is huge issue when it comes to the using public WiFi. The problem is that your computer has unique address, which is going to be recorded by the router of any public location. So if your address is tracked down by the router, it will lead to your location and device. The second problem with using public Wifi is common hacking attacks. Attacking public Wifi is known as man-in-the-middle, and it will compromise your anonymity. In that case, other hacker connected to the same network connection as you will be able to track you down. These are basic tips and

precautions when it comes to the anonymity while going online and staying safe and protected while hacking.

Chapter 4: How To Setup NMAP

We are already halfway; now you are familiar with the basics when it comes to the hacking. We already discussed Linux Terminal and tips and precautions for you to stay completely anonymous and protect your identity while hacking. The next thing of great importance is setting up NMAP which stand for network mapper. Network Mapper is the type of security scanner which is used in order to discover any hosts and service on the devices. A computer network is filled with anonymous hosts and services, and NMAP is tracking and discovering them and putting them together by building the certain map of network. Hence the name network mapper. In order to do this network mapper is sending special packets to the different hosts which are targets in this case and then NMAP analyzes the responses from the hosts.

Network mapping software provides many great utilities such as host discovery, operating system detection, and vulnerability detection. These are all great features for probing computer network. Besides these basic features, NMAP provides many other advanced features. Network mapper tool is constantly being developed and refined by the computer science community. Firstly it started as Linux utility, but later expanding to the other platforms such as Solaris, Windows, and IRIX. Among the IT community, NMAP utility for Linux is the most popular today and closely followed by operating system Windows.

There is no surprise that network mapper is great tool when it comes to the hacking. You should keep in mind that computer network is filled with the great number of hosts and services and network mapping is a great way to discover them all. Some of the features that network mapper provides are port scanning, determining operating system, scriptable interaction with the hosts and detection of the version meaning interrogating network services. Network mapper is used when it comes to the generating traffic to the target, finding any vulnerabilities, auditing security of your computer and analyzing open ports and preparing for auditing.

Now we should see how to setup network mapper scanning. It may sound terrifying, but it is quite easy to do, and often NMAP can be installed just by doing one command. As I said, NMAP could work on many different platforms provided with both source code compilation and installation methods.

➤ The first logical step for you is to check if you already have network mapper installed. Many platforms already have NMAP tool installed such as Linux and BSD. To find out if you already have NMAP, you should open terminal window and execute command NMAP, and if NMAP already exists, you will see that in the output. On the other hand, if you don't have NMAP installed you will see error message. In any case, you should consider having the latest version of network mapper and upgrading it.

NMAP is running from shell prompt. This is letting users to quickly execute the commands without wandering around bunch of configuration scripts and option fields. It may be intimidating for the beginners the fact that NMAP tools have a great number of command-line options even though some of them are ignored by many users such as commands for debugging. Interpreting and executing any outcome will be easy once you figure out how the command-line works and how to pick among command-line options,

➤   In case you don't have NMAP already installed, you should download one from the internet. Nmap.Org is right place for downloading hence it is official source for downloading. You can download from the Nmap.Org both source codes and binaries. Source codes will come in the shape of compressed tar files and binaries are available for many platforms including Linux and Windows.

➤   After you downloaded source codes and binaries from the Nmap.Org, you may be intimidated by the verifying the integrity of the maps downloaded. Many of the popular packages of the maps such as OpenSSH, Libpcap or Fragrouter may be easily infected with the great number of malicious trojans. The Same thing can happen to the software distribution sites such as SourceForge and Free Software Foundation. You should be careful not to download infected files.

➤ When it comes to the verifying NMAP tools, you should consult the PGP signatures that come together with the NMAP version you downloaded. When you download NMAP, you will get both PGP signatures and cryptographic hashes. You can find both in the NMAP signatures directory. The most secure way of verification of the NMAP is PSG signatures which came with the tool. Of course, you will need NMAP special signing key because NMAP versions are signed with these special keys. In order to get one visit on of the popular key servers. Once you get the special signing key, you will import it through the command, and you are only doing this once. By doing this, you are verifying all of your future releases.

It is easy when it comes to the verification with the proper signature key, and it takes single command. Besides signature keys, there are other options for verifying the NMAP like MD5 and SHA1 hashes if you are more into casual validation. But be careful, hashes from third party sites may easily be infected and corrupted. Once you verify NMAP, you can build the network of the host sand servers from the source code.

Chapter 5: Which Tools The Hackers Use To Crack Passwords

You already know who is a hacker. Hackers are using their knowledge and abilities to break into the system, to access the information and modify and create something completely new. Now it is time to see which tools the hackers use in order to break into system and to crack passwords. The first and most important thing is as I mentioned before is operating system Linux which will give you complete power when it comes to using hacking tools of any kind. There are many different types of tools for hacking, depending on the purpose and knowledge of the users. Keep in mind what type of the hacking and for which purpose you are going to do. Depending on your personal interest you may need tools for firewalls, intrusion detection systems, root kit detectors, packet crafting tools, wireless hacking or vulnerability exploitation tools. All of these tools come bundled with Linux, so I recommend Linux appropriate toolbox.

I already mentioned network mapper as a very useful hacking tool for discovering and mapping network hosts. When it comes to the cracking password, there is a great number of tools and software of great importance for the hackers.

There are many ways of cracking password depending on the tool used.

Most common ways include cracking passwords:

- with the help of brute forcing
- by using dictionary attacks cracking encrypted passwords
- with the hashes cracking windows passwords

- by analyzing wireless packets cracking of WEP or WPA passwords
- by identifying different kinds of injections and scripts and discovering hidden scripts and resources.

Here is the list of cracking password tools I would recommend.

1.   Aircrack-ng:

Aircrack-ng is really powerful cracking tool which includes analysis tool, detectors, and WPA crackers. Among these utilities, it also includes a great number of analysis tools for wireless LAN. It is working for cracking passwords with a wireless network interface. The wireless network interface has the controller which drivers support raw mode of monitoring and can take up a great traffic. The most important thing is that this tool is completely free to download and can work on any platforms including OSX, OpenBSD, and

Linux. This tool is perfect for cracking password due to its work in the field of the WiFi security. This tool focuses on the monitoring and capturing packets and exporting it to files which will be processed by the third party tools.

2.   Crowbar

This is the second great tool for cracking password used by many hackers. Crowbar is one of the most powerful brute force cracking tools. When you are using Crowbar, you have opportunity to be in the control of things submitted to web servers. Crowbar is not identifying positive responses, but it is comparing content of the responses with the baseline. Crowbar is completely free for downloading and works only with Linux operating system. Crowbar is powerful tool when it comes to the supporting role and is used during penetration tests.

3.   John The Ripper

It is s the most popular password cracking tool. It is really powerful and highly effective when it comes to the cracking, and that is why John The Ripper is the part of the huge family of hacking tools Rapid7.In the field of the cryptographic system, hackers are trying to find any vulnerabilities in the security network. Cracking password means recovering password from the data previously stored by the computer system or network. One of the most popular ways of cracking a password is known as brute-force attack in which computer simply guesses and hash the passwords. If you want to be real professional in the hacking world, you should get to know more about cryptographic science. John The Ripper can be downloaded for free online, and there is also pro version which you can buy. For cracking a password, this commercial version will be enough providing you great performance and speed.

Originally John The Ripper was developed only for Unix-like operating systems, but today it can work on different platforms. This tool is the best option when it comes to the only cracking passwords.

4.   Medusa

I can't discuss hacking tools and not to mention another great hacking tool Medusa. Medusa is also brute force tool providing users with excellent performance. The biggest advantage of this tools is thread-based testing allowing you to fight against multiple hosts and users. Medusa is developed in modular design, with great features like flexible user input and it is completely free to download. Medusa is running on Linux and MAC OS X operating systems. This tool can perform attacks with great speed against a large number of protocols such as HTTP, telnet, and databases.

Besides these tools for cracking a password, I

warmly recommend RainbowCrack, SolarWinds and THC Hydra.

Chapter 6: TOR And The DarkNet

I already mentioned TOR and some of its features which are very powerful software when it comes to the staying anonymous while hacking and being online. TOR is software that enables users anonymous communication by directing traffic on the internet through worldwide and free networks which are consisting of more thousands of relays all over the world. TOR is concealing your location from anyone online including all kinds of network surveillance and analysis of network traffic. By using TOR, you are making it harder for the internet activity to be traced back to you while you are online. You are preventing from being traced and hiding all of your instant messages, online posts and any visit to the web sites. TOR is originally developed in order to protect personal information, to give more freedom to the users and protect them while being online.

TOR is developed by encryption of the communication stack, nested like layers of the onion. It is working by encrypting a huge number of files including IP addresses multiple times and sending it to the virtual circuit. After the encryption is done and the innermost part of the encryption is sent to the final destination without revealing and knowing the source of the IP address. This is possible due to routing in the communication, and the IP address is more concealing by the hop in the TOR circuit. This method eliminates any way of communication peers being traced back to the user. Since network surveillance relies upon determining and discovering users destination and source, by using TOR software you will prevent revealing your identity and location to the network surveillance and be free from traffic analysis.

Beside Tor software the other important compound when it comes to the hacking world is DarkNet. DarkNet is special type of network, overlay networking allowing its users to access it only with special software and configuration. To enter into DarkNet network, you will also need specific authorization. DarkNet network is usually using non-standards protocols of communication and specific ports for accessing. There are two types of DarkNet networks. First one is friend –to-friend and privacy networks. A friend-to-friend network is usually used for file sharing, and TOR is the second one used as strictly privacy network.

You shouldn't mix DarkNet with the deep web. The deep web is the term referring to the all hidden parts of the internet which can't be accessed by any search engine such as Google and Yahoo. Some of the experts believe that content of the deep web is much bigger than the surface web. In fact, the deep web doesn't contain anything sinister but contain large databases and libraries which can be accessed only by members. Some of the search engines of deep web are FreeNet and TorSearch. DarkNet is just small part of the much bigger is known as for anonymous internet.

When you are surfing through DarkNet, both web surfers and publishers are completely anonymous. You will achieve anonymous communication using TOR software. When you are connected to the regular internet network, your computer accesses host server of the site you are visiting, but with the TOR software that link is broken. Your communication will be registered on the network, but TOR will prevent transport mediums from knowing who is doing communication. TOR as a part of DarkNet utility is perfect for anonymous communication and online freedom, running on most operating systems.

The DarkNet was originally developed for the military and government, and today they are mostly using the benefits of the DarkNet. Regular internet connection and network can easily discover your location, and this is the main reason for using DarkNet. It is also popular among journalists, politicians, activists and revolutionaries. Accessing the hidden contents of the internet is really easy. Like I said before, installing TOR browser will let you enter the DarkNet. Besides Tor, you can install TheFreeNet project for accessing hidden contents on the internet and allows you in creating private networks, unlike TOR. There is another privacy network I2P which stands for the invisible internet project.

For the absolute anonymity, you should use TOR or any other privacy network together with VPN and nobody will be able to see your online activities. There is no wonder why these software for privacy are really popular today. You are never too protected. You should always keep in mind that all of the search engines you are using are tracking and remembering all of your activities while being connected to the network. Surfing through the DarkNet with TOR software you are making great steps in staying anonymous and protecting your personal information.

Chapter 7: How You Can Use Multiple Tools To Gather Information With Wireless Hacking

While cracking wireless networks, hackers are attacking and defeating devices responsible for security of the network. WLANs is wireless local-area network known as WiFi. WLANs are extremely vulnerable due to the security holes. Wireless hacking is direct attract and intrusion, and there are two main problems when it comes to the wireless security. The first problem is due to the weak configuration and secondly is due to weak encryption.

You should keep in mind that hacking attack is hard job, step by step procedure. Hackers are using many techniques and strategies in order to get full access. You will need to know many combinations and methods in order to break into the security through security holes. Every wireless network is potential hole as well as wired network. Real hackers must rely on their knowledge in computer science, physical skills, social engineering and any other work that involves interaction between people.

When it comes to the wireless hacking, there are plenty of options available. Here is the list of options:

1.   **Aircrack:** It is not only one of the most powerful tools; it is also one of the most popular ones for wireless hacking. Aircrack is developed for using the best algorithms in order to recover passwords by discovering and tracking down packets. Once the packet is captured Aircrack will try to recover the password. In order to attack with greater speed, it implements standard FMS attack with better optimization. There are great online video tutorials how to use Aircrack tool, and it is running on the

Linux operating system. If you are using Aircrack on the Linux, it will require more knowledge of Linux.

2. **Airsnort:** It is another great and powerful tool for wireless hacking besides Aircrack. Airsnort is a powerful tool used for decrypting any WEP wireless network encryption. The best thing is that Airsnort is completely free to download and is running both on Linux and Windows operating systems. Airsnort works in the way of monitoring computing keys and transmissions when it has enough packets previously received. Due to its simple use, this tool is perfect for beginners.

3. **Kismet:** It is another great tool used by a great number of people for wireless hacking. This one is the wireless network sniffer. Kismet is working with any

wireless card and supports rfmon mode as well. Kismet is working by collecting and receiving packets passively and identifying hidden networks. You can download it for free, and it is available for many platforms including Linux, OSX, and BSD.

4. **NetStumbler**: It is wireless hacking tool used worldwide by a huge number of people. NetStumbler is running only on the Windows operating system and can be downloaded for free. There is also mini version of NetStumbler available called MiniStumbler. This tool is mainly developed for war driving and discovering unauthorized access points. There is great disadvantage when it comes to this tool. It can easily detect by the most intrusion systems which are available today. Besides this, the tool is working poorly running on the64bit

Windows operating system. NetStumbler is working by actively collecting useful information from the network.

5. **inSSIDer:** It is one great and popular wireless scanner for Windows operating system. This tool was originally free to download but became premium, so you will have to pay in order to get inSSIDer tool. Among many tasks that this tool can perform the most important are finding open wireless access points and saving logs from by the GPS.

6. **WireShark:** It is really powerful tool used as network analyzer. With WireShark, you will be able to see what is happening in your personal network. With this tool, you can easily live capture and analyze any packets. You can check a large number of data fast and at micro-

mode. It is working on many platforms including Solaris, Windows, FreeBSD, Linux and many other. In order to use WireShark, you have to be familiar with network protocols.

7. **coWPAtty:** It is a perfect tool when it comes to the automated dictionary attacking. It is running only on the Linux operating system. With the command line interface containing a word lists with the passwords for executing the attack. This tool is perfect for the beginners, but disadvantage is that tool is slow in the process. Dictionary is used for cracking passwords, cracking the each word that is contained in the dictionary.

8. **Airjack:** It is wireless cracking tool with wide range of people using it. Airjack is running as packet injection tool, hence

the name Airjack. This tool is making network go down by injecting packets.

Other than the tools, I mentioned here, and I also recommend you other tools such as WepAttack, OmniPeek, and CloudCracker.

Chapter 8: How To Keep Yourself Safe From Being Hacked

In this last chapter, we should discuss how to stay safe and not get hacked. Hackers can break into your personal computer network if you are not careful. They can steal your personal information. You should be careful when it comes to your digital life and take some precautions before going online and compromising yourself to the world. You should keep in mind that professional hackers can have bad purposes, can steal your bank accounts, your personal emails, and social media accounts as well. Keeping yourself from being hacked is of great importance for safe and protected digital life.

➤ Be Careful about what you Share Online

First and the most important thing is to be careful what you share online. Posting online info which is usually asked as security questions are not good idea. All of this information can be used by hackers to break into your personal accounts. Hackers are able to steal millions of password and personal files, causing blackouts. These tips are of great importance for not letting that happen to you.

➤ **Setting Strong and Unique Passwords**

You should always use strong and unique password. By adding extra level of protection known as two-factor authentication, you are making yourself more protected. By enabling two-factor, you are going to need something more besides password to log into your account. Often it is numerical code which is sent to your cellphone.

➤ Download a Password Manager Tool

Before going online, I recommend you to download a password manager tool, which is going to save all of your passwords. I recommend you to download Dashlane or 1Password.

➤ Use LittleSnitch

I previously mentioned you should use virtual private network that will prevent intruders from entering into your personal network by routing the internet traffic. Another great software for staying safe while being connected to the network is LittleSnitch which monitors all of your outgoing connections. It will alert you whenever computer is trying to send files to the unknown server. Your laptop should be using full disk encryption, if not you should turn it on.

➤ Don't Underestimate the Importance of Antivirus Programs

You should keep in mind the importance of antivirus programs. And yes, it is true that antivirus are basically full of security holes, but still having an antivirus program installed is a good idea for staying protected from trojans. Besides using antiviruses, I recommend using simple security plugins such a sad blockers.

➤ Stop Using Flash

If you are using flash, you should know that flash is the most insecure software with a great number of security holes perfect for hackers.

➤ Backup Your Files Regularly

Finally, yet importantly, the last

recommendation is to back up your files regularly. You should back up your files usually when you are disconnected from the network. You should use external hard disk in case you get ransom ware.

You should never underestimate potential danger and threat. Hackers are always lurking new victims, take these precautions for staying safe and protected while being online. These tips can be life changing when it comes to the digital life and online freedom.

Conclusion

Here we are at the end of the road. We discussed basics when it comes to the hacking with step by step guides. I think now you are ready to do some real hacking job. Now you are familiar with tools of great importance for hacking, using Linux Terminal is no foreign to you, you are able to crack some serious wireless network connections and be protected while wandering through the internet. Like I said before you should keep in mind that hacker job is going to take many sacrifices and it will cost you many sleepless nights. I don't want to discourage you, and you just need to be prepared in every possible way.

Learning and expanding your limits is the most essential when it comes to the hacking. Knowledge will get you on the right path and secure you successful job. Now you have considerable amount of knowledge in hacking to start with real cracking and hacking. You know there is enormous amount of knowledge out there on the computers, and there is no possible way for single person to access it all and learn everything. You will eventually figure out in which field of computer science are you interested the most. Maybe you are mostly interested in software development or computer security, in both cases, you will need to know basics in order to improve your skills and upgrade your knowledge.

Hacking is knowing what is going on inside the network and computer and understanding all of the processes happening inside the devices. By knowing what is going on inside the computer and breaking into the system, you will be able to modify information you accessed and create something completely new. By accessing and breaking into huge databases and libraries, you will have all of the information you need. You will have the real power in your hands. And for the end, you should keep in mind that only ethical and moral hacking is for good purposes. You just need to dedicate your work towards ethical purposes.

In order to get the most out of this book we have included a FREE BONUS on the next page. This will help increase your understanding of Hacking and overall computer programming.

Computer Programming Language: The Blueprint

Learn the Basics of Computer Programming Languages

By: Cyber Punk Architects

Introduction

Working in coding can be a great thing to learn. It allows you to learn more about how your own computer works and can be a fantastic way to keep it safe and make some of your own programs. Too many people assume that computers and the programming that goes with them are just going to be too hard for them to learn without them having years of experience or school, but the reality is, anyone is able to learn a coding language, you just need to pick one and get started.

This guidebook is a great resource to help you to get started with some of the most popular coding languages that are in use right now. We will start out with some of the basics of computer programming and why you would want to learn one of these languages, before moving on to the basics of starting with this one and how to make it work for your needs. Some of these are great all on their own, and some will be better when you combine them with another coding language to get even better results.

Inside this guidebook, we are going to learn some of the best coding languages, some of the most popular, which will help you to get started on the right track. Inside we are going to look at some of the basics, and how to write your first codes, for some of the most popular coding languages including C#, C++, Python, Java, and JavaScript. With these basic coding languages you will be able to work on almost any of the coding languages that you would like including making your own websites and other programs.

When you are ready to learn a bit more about some of the best coding languages out there and you want to get started on your own, make sure to check out this guidebook and see how

easy it can be to get started on some of the best
coding languages from above.

Chapter 1: Why Learn About Computer Programming

Computer programming is a great skill to learn how to use. Most people are worried that computer programming is going to be too hard for them to learn. They feel that unless they spend a lot of time learning the computer or having to spend years at school in order to do anything. But even as a beginner, it is easy to learn how to work with computer coding. In the following chapters, we are going to talk about some of the basic coding languages that are really popular and will help you to learn how to get started and you will be able to see how easy computer programming can be.

You don't have to do something that is too complicated when you are getting started. You won't have to know how to hack onto some of the other computer systems or create operating systems or anything like that when you are first getting started. If you want to get to that later on, it is something that you can work with, but for now, some of the basics are all that you need to get started and have a good time. Let's take a look at some of the reasons that you would want to learn how to work on computer programming before we move on to some of the best coding languages that you can use to get the most out of your new coding skills.

Make your own programs

One of the best options that you can do when it comes to using a new coding language is that you are able to make some of your own codes. Each of the coding languages will have their own options when it comes to what you are able to create. For example, C# is a more advanced option that can handle some of the bigger projects that you want to work on while Python is good for those who are beginners and Java and JavaScript are great for when you want to work on your own websites and the add-ons that come with them.

You will find that there are so many programs that you are able to make when it comes to a coding language and you are able to design almost anything that you would like.

One good idea to work with is to make sure that you figure out what kinds of projects that you would like to work on and then figure out what coding language that you would like to work on to make that project a reality. The only limitation is your imagination when it comes to the things that you are able to create.

Answer questions when things go wrong

No matter what kind of computer you have, there are always times when something will go wrong. The computer could run into an issue with a new program that you are working on or it may get a virus or another issues. Sometimes the computer gets old and just needs a little bit of extra help compared to some of the others.

When these things go wrong, many times we are going to try to find a computer professional and pay them a lot of money in order to get them all fixed up. We get the problem fixed in this manner usually, but we have no idea of the type of issue that was going on or even how it was fixed in the first place. This is fine for some people, but wouldn't it be nice if we were able to understand what is going on with our computers and even how to fix them ourselves?

When you learn a bit about coding, you may be able to fix some of the issues on your own. You will be able to use some of the coding to take a look through the issue that is coming up on your screen and make some changes. You maybe will be able to figure out that the new program you installed is not the best one for your particular computer program, perhaps you placed something in the wrong order, or you can make some simple changes.

The coding that you will learn may not be able to fix all of the issues that come up, but you will find that it can make a bit difference in how well you can take care of and fix the issues on your computer.

Learn more about computers

Even if you don't have any ideas for programs in mind right now, it is still a great idea to work with a new coding language. You are going to be surprised by how much it is able to teach you about your own computer.

These coding languages are going to help you to manipulate and change around the things that are going on in your computer, whether you are trying to look things up or to make a new program. In this guidebook, many of the programs that we are going to do concentrate on the Hello World program to get started, so that you can get used to them and you get to see how your computer will react to each of the codes.

Many times we are going to get into a new coding language and be uncertain about what we are doing. Most of us have not spent the last many years working in computers and making them our own. But with the help of a new coding language and learning something new, we will learn so much great stuff about how our computers work.

Chapter 2: The C# Programming Language

The first language we are going to work with is the C# programming language. This is a very popular coding language, but it is considered an intermediate one to learn. You will like that there is a lot of power that comes with this coding language and it is very easy to learn how to use and create your programs from. To get started with some of these options, make sure to visit this website to download the C# language: http://www.microsoft.com/en-us/download/details.aspx?id=7029

What are the variables?

When we bring up the topic of variables in our code, we are talking about the names that we give to all the data that is inside our programs; these data types are ones that we want to store for now but which we may want to manipulate a bit later on. For example, if you want to store the age of your user inside of the program, you would need to name the data, using the userAge, and then declare that this is a variable userAge with the following statement:

int userAge:

This declaration statement will be used in order to state the data type that is going with the variable and then the name as well as the data type will refer to any data that is stored inside of the variable (which depending on the code can be either some text or a string of numbers). Since we used the variable (int) for this example, the code is going to show that there will be an integer inside, which is something that works since we want to get an age, or a number. After you take the time to declare the variable of userAge, the program will save some space in the memory of your computer so that this data can be stored. You can come back and find this variable later on and access any of the data, even making some modifications, simply by using the right name later on.

The data you will see inside of C#

When it comes to picking out the data types, there are some variety that comes with this kind of language. Some of these we are going to talk about throughout the book because they are common and will work on many of the codes that we are trying to write. Some of the most common data types that are found in this language include:

Int: this is the one that will stand for integer. It is going to be a number of some sort, as long as it doesn't have a decimal or a fraction in it. Char: this is the one that will stand for character. It is a single unit inside of the code and it can be used in order to store that single character. You can add together characters inside the code to get what you would like.

Bool: this one is going to stand for Boolean and it is based off the idea of being either true or false. It is often used to help out with control flow statements and will check to see whether your answer is true or false based on the conditions that you are using.

String: this is the one that is used any time that you would like to create, manipulate, or even compare different pieces of text that are inside of the code.

Another data type that you will probably utilize a lot when working in C# includes the operator. These operators are really busy in the code because they are responsible for doing so many different things. They can assign a value to whatever variable you are working on, they can compare different variables to see if they are alike or different, and they can even do some mathematical equations for you. There is just so much that the operators are going to be able to do to help you out. Some of the different types of operators that you can work with include:

Arithmetic Operators

The arithmetic operators are responsible for helping you to do various mathematical equations. If you need to add a few variables together or do something else similar, these are the ones that you will need to work with. Some of the arithmetic operators that you are able to choose from include:

(+): this is the addition operator.
(-): this is the subtraction operator
(*): this is the multiplication operator
(/): this is the operator for division
(%); this is the modulo operator
(++): this is the increment operator and is used to increase the value of your operand by one.

(--): this is the decrement operator and it is used in order to decrease your operands value by one.

One thing to remember when working on your code is that you are able to use multiple of these inside of the same part. You can add together more than two numbers or you can do a combination and add together a few numbers before subtracting others and so on. You just need to remember that the order of operations is going to come into play here and the system is going to go in a certain manner in order to get the right answer. It is going to first multiply, and then divide, and then move on to addition and subtraction, going from left to right, to get the correct answer.

Relational operators

Next on the list is the relational operators. These are the ones that will compare whether the two operands you have are equal or not equal and then give you the right result at the end. The most common types of relational operators that you may find include:

(==): this is the equal to operator. If the two values are equal, you will get a true result.
(!-): this operator is the not equal operator.
(>): this is the greater than operator.
(<): this is the less than operator.
(<=): this is less than or equal to.
(>=): this is greater than or equal to.

When you are working on the relational operators, you are working with the Boolean data type. This means that the result you are getting will be either true or false. If the answer gives you a return of true, it means that the statement that is connected to your code is going to be executed. But if it ends up that the statement is false, the code is going to end; if you set up a conditional statement, it will be the second statement that releases if your answer returns a false.

Logical operators

There are several logical operators that you will be able to use inside of your C# code including;

(&&): this is the logical AND. It is only going to show up as true if both of your operands are true.
(||): this is the logical OR. This operator is going to give you true for an answer if at least one of your operands ends up being true.
(^): this is the logical exclusive OR and it will result in a true if one of your operators is true.
(!): this one will be able to reverse the value of the Boolean variable.

These are similar to the relational operator because it is also going to be seen as a Boolean answer. Your return is going to be either true or false and depending on the conditions that you set up, you will be able to get the right statements to show up on the screen.

Working on Your First Code

Here we will need to open up the compiler for C# and get started on our very first code. Here is what we will need to write out to get that to work:

using System;

using System.Collections.Generic;

using SystemLinq;

using System.Text;

using System.Threading.Tasks;

namespace HelloWorld

{

  //A simple program to display the words Hello World

```
class Program
{
        static void Main(string[] args)
        {
                Console.WriteLine("Hello
World!");
                Console.Read();
        }
}
}
```

As you work on this code, you may see that
while you are typing, there is sometimes a box
that appears that will provide you with tips or
other help. This is the Intellisense part that
comes with the VSC compiler and it is good for
beginners who need some help with the code
they are writing. If you are uncertain that you
are writing the code properly or you don't know
what you should write out next, this is a good
thing to look for. Once you have this code typed
into the compiler, you can push on the Start

button on your menu so that the program is executed.

If you have some trouble getting the VSC running, you will see that the compiler will provide you with the "Output Window" error. You will be able to push on the error to see what it is and make the changes that are needed before running the program.

Now, if you wrote the code properly, and the program doesn't bring up any other issues, you should have a little black window that comes up on your screen that says "Hello World" inside. When you see this and are satisfied with the work, you will can exit out of this by pressing the Enter key. And now you are done with the first program you need for C#.

Chapter 3: The C++ Programming Language

The C++ language is another one that you may want to add into the mix when you are learning ow to work with the coding languages. It is simple to learn and you are going to love some of the results that you get. It is a bit easier to learn compared to the C# language and it provides you with many great programs that you are going to love. Before getting started, make sure to visit https://www.microsoft.com/en-us/download/details.aspx?id=5555 to get it ready for your computer. Let's take a look at some of the great things that you are able to do with this coding language.

The Hello World Program

Now that you have had some time to set up

your environment, it is time to work on your first code and learn how to write a program in this language. We are going to work on the Hello World code and see how easy it is to write out the first code inside this language. In order to get the screen to print out Hello World, you would need to type in the following:

```
#include <iostream>
using namespace std;

//main() is where program execution begins

int main()
{
        cout <<"Hello World"; //prints Hello World
        return 0;
}
```

Now that we have written out the code, we need to look at all the parts to learn what they mean.

First, C++ will involve a variety of headers which are used to hold onto useful information and data for the program. The <iostream> header is the one required for this code. We then moved on to adding in the line "using namespace std". At this area, we are telling the compiler which namespace to bring up your information.

The int main() part is going to tell the program that this is the primary function where the program should start being executed and the two slashes are comments that let other programmers know what you are doing in the code without effecting how well the code works. All of this is going to come together in order to print off "Hello World" onto the screen.

Comments in the Code

Comments are important when working inside of the C++ coding language. These are going to help you to explain certain parts of the code to the other programmers who may be looking through the code or can even be used as a way to name your new code. If you use the right symbols inside of the comment, the compiler is just going to skip right over the comment so any comments that you write out won't mess up the code or change anything.

If you would like to write out a comment inside of your code, you would need to use the /* at the beginning of the code and then the */ at the end of the code to show the compiler that you are done writing out the comment at this point.

C++ Variables

When we are working inside of C++, a variable is going to give you a name for the storage of data inside of the program. Each of the variables that you have inside of the C++ program is going to have a specific type, even with this particular code that you are working on. The variable is going to also work to determine the size as well as the layout of the memory for the variable and the range of values that you can store inside of the memory.

When it comes to naming the variables, you will be able to use the underscore character, digits, and letters in order to get it named right, but you will need to make sure that the beginning is either an underscore or a letter rather than a number. There are many variables that you will be able to use, but the most common types include:

Bool: this is going to store values of false or true.
Char: this is going to usually just be one letter or number and it is considered a type of integer.
Int: this is often considered the natural size of the integer.

Void: this is the one that you will use if there is an absence of a type in your code.

You will want to declare your variables so that the compiler knows that there is one present and is able to know the type and the name before proceeding. The variable declaration will have meaning only when it is compiled because the compiler will actually need a definition of the variable when it is time to link them up. If you are using several files in order to define the variable, you will need to go through a variable declaration. The extern keyword is the best for helping to declare the variable at any place that you want in the code.

A good example of writing out a variable inside this language includes the following;

#include <iostream>
using namespace std;

114

```cpp
// Variable declaration:
extern int a, b;
extern int c;
extern float f;

int main () {
   // Variable definition:
int a, b;
int c;
float f;

   // actual initialization
   a = 10;
   b = 20;
   c = a + b;

cout<< c << endl ;

   f = 70.0/3.0;
cout<< f << endl ;

   return 0;
```

}

Chapter 4: The Python Programming Language

Python is considered one of the best coding languages if you are a beginner. It is really easy to use and can even be combined with a lot of the other coding languages if you are looking on getting started and want to add in some more power along the way. It is one of the best and has a huge support group to help you out with any of the programs that you want to create. To get the Python language on your computer, visit www.python.org/downloads

There are so many things that you are able to do in order to get a code up and running on Python. Many people may avoid using Python because they think that it is too simple or it just isn't going to get the job done. But in reality, it is simple just for the fact that even a beginner is able to learn how to use it, but that doesn't mean that you aren't able to do a lot with it. This chapter is going to take some time to look at the different commands that you can do with Python programming in order to make your programs and codes come to life.

Variables

Variables may sound like something that is too complicated to learn, but they are basically locations in the memory that are reserved in order to store the values of your code. When you work on creating a variable, you are reserving this spot in the memory. In some cases, the data type that is in the variable will tell the interpreter to save the memory space and can even decide what you are able to store on your reserved memory.

Assigning values to your variables

The value is going to be one of the basic things

that your program will need to work with. It can be a string, such as Hi World, 3.14, which is considered a type float, or a whole number like 1, 2, and 3 which is considered an integer. Python variables will not need an explicit declaration in order to reserve the space in the memory that you need. This is something that is going to happen automatically whenever you place a value with the variable. For this to work, simply place the (=) so that the value knows where it is supposed to go.

Some examples of this include:

X = 10   *#an integer assignment*
Pi = 3.14   *#a floating point assignment*
Y= 200   *#an integer assignment*
Empname = "Arun Baruah"   *#a string assignment*

Keep in mind that when you are working on codes, you are able to leave a comment with your wok by using the # sign. This allows you to explain what is going on in the code, leave some notes, or do something else within the program. It is not going to be read by the interpreter since it is just a little note that you are leaving behind for yourself or for someone else.

The next part is going to depend on which version of Python you are using. Python 2 is fine with you writing out print and then the information you want to talk about but Python 3 is going to require you to place the parenthesis in to make it work. An example would be:

Print("y = %d" %y)
Print("x = %d" %x)
Pring("Employee Name is %s" %empname)

These would then be put through the interpreter and the outputs that you would get should be

X = 10

Y = 200

Employee Name is Arun Baruah

Now go through and put in this information to your program and see what comes up. If you didn't get the right answers like listed above, you should go and check that the work is done. This is a simple way to show what you are able to do with Python and get the answers that you need.

Multiple Assignments

In addition to working with the single variables that were listed above, you will also be able to work on multiple assignments. This means that you are going to be able to assign one value to several different variables at the same time. To do this, you would just need to place the equal sign between all of them to keep things organized and to tell the computer that the value is going to be with all of the variables together. You can keep them separated out if that is easier for you, but using this method is going to help you to send everything to the same memory location on the computer and will give the code a clearer look on your screen.

A good example of how to give more than one variable the same value includes:

a = b = c = 1

This is telling the code that you want all of them to be tied with the value of 1 and that all of these variables should have the same value and that you want to assign them all to the same location within your memory.

Standard Data Types

Another thing that you are able to work on

when doing Python is the various data types. These are going to be used in your code in order to define the operations that you can do on each data type as well as explain to others the storage method that will be used for this kind of data. Python has five data types that are considered standard including:

Numbers
Dictionary
Tuple
List
String
Numbers

Number data types are the ones that will store the numeric values. They are going to be created as objects once you assign a value to them. There are also four different types of numericals that Python will support including

Complex (such as complex numbers)

Float (floating point real values

Long (long integers that can also be shown as hexadecimal and octal.)

Int (signed integers)

One thing to note is that while Python will allow you to use the lowercase l when doing the long form of a number, it is best to go with an uppercase L whenever you are using the letter. This is going to help you avoid confusion in reading the program between the l and the 1 as they look really similar. Any time that Python is displaying a long integer that has the l in it, you will see the uppercase L.

Strings

Strings are identified in Python as a contiguous set of characters that will be shown by the use of quotations marks. Python is going to allow for either double quotes or single quotes, but you do need to keep things organized. This means that if you use a double quote at the beginning of your string, you need to end that same string with the double quote. The same goes when you are using a single quote. Both of these will mean the same thing, you just need to make sure that you are using the proper quote marks to make the code look good and to avoid confusing the Python program.

In addition to being able to print off the string that you would like, you are also able to tell the program to print just part of the string using some special characters. Let's look at some of the examples of what you are able to do with the strings, and the corresponding signs that you will use at well, to help illustrate this point.

```
str = 'Hi Python!'
print(str)      #prints complete string
print(str[0])  #prints the first character of the
string
print(str[2:5])        #prints characters starting
```

from the 3rd to the 5th

print(str[2:]) #prints string starting from the 3rd character

print(str*2)   #prints the string two times

print(str+"Guys")   #prints concatenated string

For the most part you are probably going to want to print out the whole string to leave a message up on your program so the first print that you do is going to be enough. But if you just want to print out Hi or some other variation of the words above, you may find that the other options are really useful. You can do any combination of these, they are just examples to help you get started!

Lists

 Lists are one of the most versatile data types that you can work on in Python. In this language, the list is going to contain different items that are either enclosed with the square brackets or separated out with commas.

They are similar to the arrays that you would see in C if you've worked with that program. The one difference that comes up with these is that the items that are in a list can be from different data types.

The values that are stored inside the list can be accessed with a slice operator as well as the [:} symbol with the indexes starting at 0 at the beginning of the list and then working down until you get to -1. The plus sign will be the concatenation operator while you can use the asterisk as the repetition operator. For some examples of what all this means and how you can use the different signs within your programming, consider some of these examples:

list = ['mainu', 'shainu', 86, 3.14, 50.2]
tinylist = [123, 'arun']

print)list)   #prints complete list

print(list[0]) #prints the first element of the list

print(list[1:3]-   #prints elements starting from the second element and going to the third

print(list [2:])   #prints all of the elements of the list starting with the 3rd element.

Print(tinylist*2)   #prints the list twice.

Print(list + tinylist) #prints the concatenated lists.

Dictionaries

Dictionaries are another kind of tool that you can use when you are working in Python. They are similar to a hash table type and they are going to work similar to the hashes or the arrays that you can find on other programming languages like C# and Perl.

They will also consist of key value pairs and while the key can be almost any type on Python, you will notice that they are usually going to be strings or numbers. For the most part, when it comes to values, you will find that they are an arbitrary object in python.

Some examples of how this will work include the following codes:

```
#dictionary stores key-value pair, later to be retrieved by the values with the keys
dict = {}
dict['mainu'] = "This is mainu"
dict[10] = 'This is number 10"
empdict = {'name': 'arun', 'code':23, 'dept': 'IT'}

print(dict['mainu']) #this will print the value for the 'mainu' key
print(dict[10])          #this will print the value for the 10 key
print(empdict)          #this will print the complete dictionary
print(empdict.keys())    #this will print out
```

all of the keys
print(empdict.values())   #this will print all
the values

One thing to keep in mind is that these dictionary values are not going to be stored in an order that is sorted. They aren't going to have the concept of ordering among the elements. This does not mean that you can say that the elements are out of order, they are just going to be unordered.

Keywords

Most of the types of programming languages that you will deal with will have some keywords or words that are reserved as part of the language. These are words that you really shouldn't use in your code unless you absolutely can't help it.

There are 33 keywords found in the most recent

version of Python and you will need to spell them properly if you want them to do the job that you lay out. The 33 keywords that you should watch out for include:

False

Class

Finally

Is

Return

None

Continue

For

Lambda

Try

True

Def

From

Nonlocal

While

And

Del

Global

Not

Yield

As

Elif

If

Or

Assert

Else

Import

Pass

Break

Except

In

Raise

Keep this list on hand if you are worried about learning the language. It will be able to help you out any time that you have issues with the interpreter about the names that you are giving the variable. You may be confused about why it is giving you some issues with the words you chose, you can go through with this list and see if you used one of the keywords inappropriately within your code.

Statements

When you are writing your code in the Python language, you are going to be making expressions and statements to get it done. Expressions are going to be able to process the objects and you will find them embedded within your statements.

A statement is basically a unit of code that will be sent to the interpreter so that it can be executed. There are two types of statements that you can use; assignment so far and print.

You will be able to write out the statement, or multiple statements, using the Python Shell to do so interactively or with the Python script using the .py extension that we talked about later.

When you type these statements into the interactive mode, the interpreter will work to execute it, as long as everything is properly in place, and then you can see the results displayed on the screen. When there are quite a few lines that you need to write in code, it is best to use a script that has a sequence of statements. A good example of this is:

```
#All of these are statements
X = 56
Name = "Mainu"
Z = float(X)
Print(X)
Print(Name)
Print(Z)
```

Operands and operators

There are a lot of great symbols that are going

to show up when you make a code in your Python program. It is important to understand what parts you are able to work with and what they are all going to mean. Operators are often used to mean subtraction, addition, division, and multiplication. The values of the operator will be called operands. You can use many different signs for these in order to get the values that you would like to see.

While you are using the operators and operands, you need to remember that there is going to be an order of evaluation that is followed. Think about going back to math class and how this all worked. You had to look for specific signs in order to figure out which tool you were supposed to use in order to come up with the right answer. This is the same when using these operands within your code.

When you have more than one of these operators in the expression, you will need to do the order of evaluation based on the rules of precedence. For anything that is arithmetic, Python is going to use the acronym PEMDAS which is parenthesis, exponentiation, multiplication, division, addition, and subtraction. If there are a number of these that are the same, such as two sets of numbers that need to be multiplied together, you will need to work from left to right to get the correct number.

Another important operator that you should look for is the modulus operator. This one is going to work with integers and is going to yield the remainder once the first operand has been divided by the second one.

Chapter 5: Working with the C Coding Language

Working with the C language is pretty simple. You can write a code that just has one line or you can go on and write a nice long one that is going to be more complex and could run a game or some other process. While you can get more complex later on, I am going to look at some of the basics of writing inside of the C language to help you to get comfortable. A good place to start when looking for downloading the C language (and to get Visual Studio with it which is one of the best), includes:
https://www.visualstudio.com/vs/

Writing a Dummy Code

First, let's take a look at writing out your dummy code. This isn't going to bring you an output like some of the other codes that we will discuss later on, but it will help you to get the hang of creating and saving a code in the C language so you are ready for the things we do later on.

So to start, you need to go into the Code Blocks IDE, or whichever IDE that you chose, and click on the New Button. You will want to open up an Empty File. Now you will need to type in a code into the editor so that you are able to create a code to save. I am going to keep this simple and just type in one line like the following:

```
main() {}
```

Now you will need to save the source file and you can do this by clicking on the Save button. You can either let this save on the default of your computer or you can choose the folder that you would like all of these code files to be saved on your computer; the choice is up to you, just remember where you are saving all of these so if you need to find them later.

Make sure to name the file something that you will be able to remember later on, or you will get confused as you start to add on more of these files over time. I am going to call this file "dummy.c". Once you have saved this, the source code file is created and it has been saved on your computer. Now you will click on the Build button.

You will notice that the code is not going to compile. What you are going to see is the minimum of the C program, which is also called the dummy. All of your codes in C need to have the main function because this is where the execution of the program is going to start; you will just need to put the main function inside of the curly brackets.

Since this is a dummy source code and one where we are just experimenting a little bit, I didn't have us put any code into the curly brackets. When you try to run this option, you will not get an output because nothing was placed inside. We will be able to add in different things later on and create an output based on what is inside the code. You may see a compiler warning when entering the dummy code, but this is not critical. You will just click on your Run button and then find that it is not able to give you any output.

Congratulations! You have just written your very first code using the C programming language. If you didn't get any output, you did the code right. This is just the basic form of writing a code in the C language and there is so much more that you are able to add into the code. Some of the other basic parts that you can add into your code includes:

Structure
Variables and values

Operators

Functions

Keywords

I am going to take you through how some of
these work so you can learn how to make the
code shine the way that you would like.

Writing Another Code

Now that I have had some time to explain a few
of the basic parts of code writing, let's take a
look at how this would work by bringing out
our dummy.c program from earlier. Just open
up the code from wherever you stored it before
and I am going to make the main function be
defined as an integer function. This basically
means that it is going to return an integer value
onto the operating system. We will need to do
some editing in order to make this happen.

Inside of your editor, you will need to add in

the keyword "int" before your "main" part to ensure that you are getting the integer output that you would like. Make sure that you place a space between both of these keywords to help the compiler to read through both of them. So to start, type out the following code:

```
int main()
{
}
```

You will notice that the code is a bit different than we originally wrote out with the first code, but putting the curly brackets in this manner is what most veteran programmers prefer to use. Now it is time to add in a statement to this main function so that it will actually show you an output. I will keep it simple and just add in the number three.

You will first need to type in the "return" and then the number three. I will write out the example of the syntax that you would use to make this happen:

```
int main()
{
        return(3);
}
```

Make sure to add in the semicolon after the statement. Save the file and then click on the Build button. As long as you type in the code like I wrote above, you shouldn't have any issues with errors or messages coming up for you. Click on the Run Button.

When using a Linux or Mac system, it is possible that you won't see any output other than the build log, and it will say that the program terminated with a status of zero. On a PC computer, the terminal window is going to show you the return value 3.

Any time that you want to add in an output to your dummy program, you need to bring in the output function. The keywords in the C language aren't going to output anything because they are just basic vocabulary, such as the words int and return. You can do this by using the "puts" command inside the program.

Let's take a look at how this is going to work when you write out some code. Make sure that the function of the "puts" is inside of parenthesis and that you place in a string of text between a double quote to make it work properly. Here is the example I am going to use:

```
int main()
{
    puts("I am the King of the C programming world");
        return 3;
}
```

When you save this source code and then click on Build, you should see a warning come up on your computer. Even if you don't see this, you need to realize that you have another step to do at this point. Before the puts function is going to work, it needs to have a definition inside, or you will find that the compiler is confused. The definition of your puts will be in the I/O header file and you need to place this into the source code with the help of the preprocessor directive.

Here is an example of how that would look inside of your code to keep things organized and to avoid errors.

```
#include<stdio.h>

int main()
{
        puts("I am the King of the C
```

programming world");

```
            return 3;
}
```

This version includes the preprocessor directive along with the definition for the puts function. You can save the file and then click on the Build and Run buttons that are at the top of the editor. If everything is typed properly, you can avoid errors and in the output terminal window, the statement that you wrote out for the puts function as well as the value 3 will show up on the screen.

Learning some of the basics of writing a code in the C language can make it easier to understand what is going on. I showed you a few of the options that you have when working inside of the C language, but there is still so much more that you are able to do. Take some time to get familiar with how these codes work, play around with the IDE and the compiler, and get comfortable before moving on and learning some more complex options when writing your own code.

Chapter 6: The JavaScript Programming Language

JavaScript is a good coding language to learn if you want to work on a website or online. This one often goes with the Java program, remember that these two are separate, in order to add some little add-ins into the whole program. It is really easy to learn and can make all the difference in how your program is going to work. Let's take a look at how the JavaScript program will work as you first get started.

Getting Started on JavaScript

The first thing we will need to do here is download the JavaScript language by visiting www.javascriptlint.com/download.htm. JavaScript is a versatile coding language that you are able to inject anywhere you would like in your page. As long as you have the HTML tags <script>...</script> around what you would like to insert. But in most cases, you will be recommended to place the script that you want to use in between the head sections or the <head>...</head> tags.

When the browser is taking a look at the content on the page, or the HTML on the page, it is going to just read through the whole thing like reading through a book. But when the browser program comes to the <script> tag, it will start to interpret whatever you have written between these tags and won't stop until it reaches the </script> part of the tag. This allows the program to interpret what you would like to have on the page in any location that you would like.

When working with the script tag, you will be able to give them one of two attributes including:

Language—this is the attribute that will specify what kind of scripting language you are using. The value for the JavaScript language is basically "javascript." If you are using a newer version of HTML, this is something that been phased out so you may not have to worry about it at all.

Type—this is the attribute that will indicate the scripting language that you are using and the value that you are using with it will be set to text/javascript when in the JavaScript language.

Writing a program

At this point you may be a bit confused on what is going on and what all of these things mean. Let's take a chance to open up the html file (use the steps that were in the first chapter if you don't already have this opened up) and then we can get started at writing your first JavaScript program. To do this, just use the code that is below:

```
<!DOCTYPE html>
<html>
<head>
<meta charset- "ISO-8859-1">
<title> My First JavaScript Program </title>
</head>
<body>
      <script language = "javascript"
type = "text/javascript">
      document.write("Welcome to
JavaScript First Program");
      </script>
</body>
</html>
```

This may seem like a lot of information to put into the code, but it is going to ensure that you are getting everything in that is needed to make a great code that others can read through. Let's separate each of the parts out to help you understand what is going on a bit better!

Explaining the code

In this code, the JavaScript code was inserted between the <body> ... </body> tags in the HTML. The code was first declared with the right attributes and then with using the document object you were able to write out the message that helped to welcome others on to the webpage. So when this is executed, the webpage should have the words "Welcome t JavaScript First Program" right at the top.

Output

When you take the HTML program that we just wrote up and try to execute it, the results that you will get would be:

Welcome to JavaScript First Program.

This is basically what you told the computer system to write so if you have put everything into their right spaces within the code that you were writing, this is the exact phrase that should show up when you are working on the code.

Line breaks and white spaces

When it comes to having spaces in your code, or even line breaks, you can use them as much as you would like. These can often help to clear up what you are writing and you won't have to worry about the code getting too long or too hard to read. That being said, it really doesn't matter how much, if any, space that you put into the code. The browser parser is not going to read these spaces so you can write out the code in the way that works for you.

This makes it easy for you to create the

indentation, lines, and other parts that you need in order to make sense of the program, to help format it properly, and to keep it looking nice. Just because the lines and the spaces aren't recognized in JavaScript does not mean that you should completely ignore them in the process.

When you are first getting started with this language, it may be a good idea to add in a few more line breaks and indents to your code. This is going to make it a bit easier to read through and you can catch some of the mistakes a bit easier. The extra white spaces aren't going to change how the system will read through the information, but it can make it easier for you to read the code and for other beginners to know what you are trying to write out.

Using semicolons

For the most part, you will end all of your

statements using the semi-colon when you are in JavaScript. These are optional if you are placing the statements on different lines from each other so the choice is really up to you. If you just write out the code with everything on one line as a continuous string, you will need to add in the semicolon but if you are separating out the statements as you go onto different lines, it is your choices whether you would like to use them. It is considered good programming practice to have them there regardless, but the program will work whether you place them there or not. The codes that we have in this guidebook will use the semicolons to help keep things clear.

Case sensitivity

You will notice that JavaScript is one of the languages that is sensitive to the cases that you are using. This means that you need to keep your use of uppercase and lowercase letters consistent throughout the program. This is true for everything that you label including identifiers, function names, variables, and keywords. For example, when you are using JavaScript, LEARN and learn will be different when the programming language is going through it.

This is important to remember when you are naming your functions and statements. If you name one of them JAVASCRIPT and then try to search for it or bring it back out by using the JavaScript word, you are going to get an error sign. You do get some say in what you name them, but try to keep all of the names for the code consistent so that you name them the same way and can easily call them back up when they are needed.

Writing comments

There are times when you will need to write out

a comment in JavaScript. You may want to tell someone else a bit more about the program or you are interested in explaining what should be placed in each of the statements. There are a few comment styles that are followed when you are using JavaScript in your coding including:

Single lines—if your comment is just going to take over one line, you simply need to use the double slash (//) to get it started.

Multiple lines—sometimes your comments will be a bit longer and they can take over a few lines. For this you will use /* to start the comment and then */. You are able to use this on single line options as well if you are worried about formatting.

JavaScript will also recognize the HTML comment if you would like to stick with this. The HTML comment is <!--. This will be treated just like a single line comment in this

language.

Closing sequence—the HTML closing sequence sign of → is not going to be recognized in JavaScript. If you would like to use this sign in your code, you will need to write it like this: //→.

When you use these options, you are telling the interpreter that it should not read the comment. You are able to put as many of these within your code as you need as long as you use the proper formatting so that the interpreter knows what you are leaving there for others and what it should leave alone. Once the comment is over, the interpreter will go back and start executing whatever else you have written in the code.

There are a lot of different times when you will need to write out a comment to help make sense of things in your code. If you want to tell someone what you are doing within the code, answer some questions, or help yourself or another coder to understand what information needs to go into the statements, these comments are great. You can add in as many of the comments as you would like, as long as you use the right signals, because the compiler will not read through them and won't try to execute them at all.

Some examples of using comments in JavaScript includes:

```
<!DOCTYPE html>
<html>
<head>
<meta charset = "ISO-8859-1">
<title>JavaScript Comments</title>
</head>
<body>
        <script type = "text/javascript">
        <!—The opening sequence single line
```

comment.

The closing sequence HTML comment//-->

```
// This is a single line comment.
/*
*This is a multiple line comment in JavaScript
*/
</script>
</body>
</html>
```

Output

When you do the program in HTML that we listed above, the output will just be blank. This is because the whole program is listed out as a comment and the interpreter is not going to lists out the comments because it has learned to not read them after the signals that we discussed above. If you had added in some other code in there, the interpreter is only going to read that and will ignore the comments that you add into the code. You are allowed to put in as many comments as you would like, as you can see from the example above, as long as you choose the right symbols to go with it so that the interpreter does not give you an error sign.

These are just some of the basic things that you need to understand in order to get started with using JavaScript on your own. Each part can help you to write out the syntax that you want and ensures that you are getting the very most out of your written code. Take some time to experiment with the comments and some of the other aspects we have discussed to figure out how these are going to work for you.

Chapter 7: Working with the Java Coding Language

While JavaScript is great at putting some of the add-ins into a website, the Java code is going to be much better for writing up the whole website or other applications that you want to use online. If you are looking to create your own personal or business website, you will want to learn how to work with the Java code. Let's take a look at some of the basics that come with this coding language and how to get started.

Writing out your code in Java

The first step that you will need to do is to download the Java coding language. You can do this by visiting https://java.com/download. Writing code can be simple inside of Java, you just need to get some experience with working inside of the system and with your text editor.

To get started with your first code inside of Java, take the following steps.

Step1: to start writing a program in Java, you will first need to set up your work environment. Open up NetBeans or whichever environment you chose for working in Java and get it ready to use.

Step 2: once the environment is up, open up your text editor that you want to use. Notepad is a good selection if you have a Windows computer, but anything that is similar will work out great.

Now we are going to create the Hello World program. This is an easy program to use on any programming language that you want to work with because you will get the hang of how the syntax works and you will get the words "Hello World" to show up on your screen.

To start this, just go to your text editor, click on new file, and then save this document as "HelloWorld.java". HelloWorld is going to be the name of your class, so keep this in mind since the class name needs to be the same as the file name.

One the file is created, it is time to declare the class and the main method. The main method will be the same in terms of method declaration no matter what kind of program you are creating inside of your Java program. At this point, you should have the following syntax:

```
public class HelloWorld {
        public static void main(String[] args) {
        }
}
```

Write this part out into your text editor. Next, you will need to write out the part of the code that will tell your text editor what you would like to have printed out. For this point, you would need to type out:

System.out.println("Hello World.");

This is going to tell the system that you want to print out the phrase "Hello World" onto the screen. You can try this out and change up the message you want to use inside of the program based on what you want to program to use. With this part, there are a few things that help to make it get done the proper way so let's take a look at how these work.

System: this part is going to alert the system that it needs to do something.

Out: this is going to tell the system that you are creating an output that you want it to print on the screen.

Println: this part will stand for print line in the system. You are basically telling the system that you want to print out the statement that comes after this part.

Parentheses: there are some parentheses that are found around the "Hello World" part. These means that the code in front of it is takin gin a parameter, or the string of Hello World.

So basically this code is working to alert the system that you need it to take some actions, that you want to create an output and that you want to print out the line "Hello World" onto your screen.

Before continuing, there are a few rules that you should follow when making these codes inside of Java. First, it is a good idea to add a semicolon at the end of the lines. This is a good programming practice and helps the text editor to print things off properly. Java is also a case sensitive language so pay attention to whether you are using upper case or lower case letters when you are writing out class names, variable names, and method names. And finally, any blocks of code that are specific to a certain loop or method will be encased with the curly brackets.

So let's put this code all together so you can place it into your text editor in the right places. public class HelloWorld {

```
    public static void main(String[] args) {
            System.out.println("Hello
World.");
    }
}
```

Once this is written into the code, it is time to save your files and then open up a command prompt, also known as a terminal, in order to compile the program. You can navigate to the folder where the HelloWorld.java is located. Type in the words javacHellWorld.java. This is going to tell your compiler that you want to compile your HelloWorld.java.

If there happen to beany errors in your code, the compiler will be able to tell you what may be wrong with your code. Otherwise, the compiler is not going to show any messages. You can then look at the directory where you store the HelloWorld.java and inside should be the HelloWorld class that we designed. This is the file that is used when you want to run your program.

Now that we have written a program, you may want to give it a try and see if this will run. Open up the terminal or the command prompt and type out java HelloWorld. This is going to tell Java that you wish to run your HelloWorld class. If everything has gone into the program properly, the statement "Hello World" will show up on the console and you have written your first code in Java!

Expanding the Hello World Program

Working with the Hello World program was pretty simple and has given you some experience with how this program is going to work. Here we are going to take the Hello World program and extend it out a bit. In the Hello World program, we printed out a string for the user to see, but now we are going to extend out the program so that the users are able to place in their name and then it will greet them by name.

First, we will import in the scanner class. In Java, there are a few libraries that you can access, but you first need to import them. One of the libraries that we need and which holds the Scanner object is the java.util. To import this Scanner class, use the following code:

import java.util.Scanner;

This tells the program that you wish to use your

Scanner object, which is inside the java.util package. Inside of the method, we will instantiate a new instance with this Scanner object. To use this Scanner class, we just need to create a new Scanner object that we are able to populate and use the methods of. To get these Scanner objects to work for us, we would need to use the following code:

```
Scanner userInputScanner = new Scanner(System.in);
```

So what does this code mean and what is it going to tell the computer to do? Here is an explanation of how the different parts move:

userInputScanner: this is the name of the Scanner object we are using. Note that this is written in what is known as the camel case; which is the conventional way of writing out your variables in Java.

the new operator will help to create a brand new instance of your object. For this instance, we created a new instance in the Scanner object with the new Scanner(System.in) part.

This new Scanner object is going to take in a parameter that will tell the object what they need scanned. The System.in is going to work for this and it tells the program that you want to scan in the input from the system, which is basically going to be the name of the user.

Now we can work on prompting the user for their input. We need to ask the user for the input so that the user has an idea that they are supposed to type something into their console. Otherwise, the program will just sit still because nothing is entered. You can accomplish this with the following code:

System.out.print("What's your name?");

The next part that you should do is ask the scanner object to take in the information that the user types and then have it store that information as a new variable. The Scanner is responsible for taking in the data that your user is typing, which should be their name at this point. To do this, use the following code:

```
String userInputName =
userInputScanner.nextLine();
```

This should tell the Scanner object that you want it to read what the user inputs into the system and use that as the variable for your next part. It can now be used as the greeting that shows back to the user. Since you have the name of the user, you can write it out so that the program mentions the name while leaving another message. The next step is to write out the following code:

```
System.out.println("hello" + userInputName +
```

"!");

At this point, we have been separating out the code to the different steps and discussing it, but let's put it all together to help you see how this code should be written out:

```
import java.util.Scanner;
public class HelloWorld (
        public static void main(String[] args) {
                Scanner userInputScanner = new
Scanner(System.in);
                System.out.print("What's your
name?");
                String userInputName =
userInputScanner.nextLine():
                System.out.println("Hello" +
userInputName + "!");
```

Once this code is in the system, you will be able to compile the program and run it. Go into your command prompt or the terminal window and then run the same commands that we did with the HelloWorld.java from the last section. You can compile this program by typing in javac HellWorld.java.

When you type in the HellowWorld.java, your program should ask "What's your Name?" You can go through and type in your name. Let's type in the name Jane. Once you press enter on this name, the program will print out Hello Jane and then the program is done.

While this part may take a few more lines to complete, it is still pretty basic. It took the original skills you learned with your first part and expanded it out into a code that has a few extra parts that come with it. Despite needing a few more parts, you will find that this is a basic code that adds in a bit more personalization to the codes you make.

And now you are set to start with the Java

program. You already know how to do two basic codes inside of this program and as you move through the other parts, you will be able to write out some more codes to get the hang of how the text editors work inside this program. (How To Write Your First JavaScript)

Conclusion

When it comes to working on some coding languages, you will find that there are so many that you are able to choose from. You may worry that it is going to be too hard to get started on a coding language that you will never be able to figure them out, but most of them are pretty easy, you just need to find the place where you are going to get started and then go from there.

This guidebook took some time to explore some of the different programming languages and how you would be able to write some of your first codes inside of them. There are quite a few computer programming languages that you are able to work with, but we took on some of the ones that are the most popular, including Python, Java, JavaScript, C# and C++. These are the ones that are the most widely used and can help you to work on so many different programs that you will be off to a great start in no time.

When you are ready to learn a bit about some of the great computer programming that you have always wanted, it is time to take a look through this guidebook and learn everything that you need about all the best coding languages!

Free Bonus!

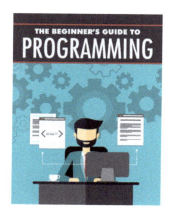

Programing can be hard but it doesn't have to be! Take this free PDF guide to understand some of the basics of programming

Download the free guide:

bit.ly/cpfreeguide

www.ingramcontent.com/pod-product-compliance
Lightning Source LLC
Chambersburg PA
CBHW041637050326
40690CB00026B/5251